EVOLVE

WORKBOOK

Samuela Eckstut

4A

CAMBRIDGE
UNIVERSITY PRESS

CAMBRIDGE
UNIVERSITY PRESS

University Printing House, Cambridge CB2 8BS, United Kingdom

One Liberty Plaza, 20th Floor, New York, NY 10006, USA

477 Williamstown Road, Port Melbourne, VIC 3207, Australia

314–321, 3rd Floor, Plot 3, Splendor Forum, Jasola District Centre, New Delhi – 110025, India

103 Penang Road, #05-06/07, Visioncrest Commercial, Singapore 238467

Cambridge University Press is part of the University of Cambridge.

It furthers the University's mission by disseminating knowledge in the pursuit of education, learning and research at the highest international levels of excellence.

www.cambridge.org
Information on this title: www.cambridge.org/9781108408745

First published 2019

20 19 18 17 16 15 14 13 12 11 10 9 8 7

Printed in Poland by Opolgraf

A catalogue record for this publication is available from the British Library

ISBN 978-1-108-40531-7 Student's Book
ISBN 978-1-108-40509-6 Student's Book A
ISBN 978-1-108-40923-0 Student's Book B
ISBN 978-1-108-40532-4 Student's Book with Practice Extra
ISBN 978-1-108-40510-2 Student's Book with Practice Extra A
ISBN 978-1-108-40925-4 Student's Book with Practice Extra B
ISBN 978-1-108-40901-8 Workbook with Audio
ISBN 978-1-108-40874-5 Workbook with Audio A
ISBN 978-1-108-41194-3 Workbook with Audio B
ISBN 978-1-108-40518-8 Teacher's Edition with Test Generator
ISBN 978-1-108-41071-7 Presentation Plus
ISBN 978-1-108-41204-9 Class Audio CDs
ISBN 978-1-108-40795-3 Video Resource Book with DVD
ISBN 978-1-108-41449-4 Full Contact with DVD
ISBN 978-1-108-41155-4 Full Contact A with DVD
ISBN 978-1-108-41417-3 Full Contact B with DVD

Additional resources for this publication at www.cambridge.org/evolve

CONTENTS

1 VOCABULARY: Describing accomplishments

A   **Circle the words to complete the phrase. One phrase has two correct answers.**

1   break *a fear /* (*a record*)
2   face *a fear / a medal*
3   get *a business / a lot of likes*
4   have *a good joke / a sense of humor*
5   rise *to a challenge / a goal for myself*
6   run *a business / a marathon*
7   set *a goal for myself / pride in something*
8   take *a medal for something / pride in something*
9   tell *a goal for myself / a good joke*
10 win *a medal / a record*
11 work *with my hands / a business*

B   **Complete the sentences with phrases from exercise 1A.**

1   When you _____run a business_____ , you organize or control a business.
2   When you _____ , you say something to make people laugh.
3   When you _____ , you create something for your job.
4   When you _____ , you get a prize in a competition.
5   When you post something online that many people think is good, you _____ .
6   When you _____ , you feel good about something you have done.
7   When you _____ , you deal with something you are afraid of.
8   When you _____ , you deal with a difficult job or opportunity successfully.
9   When you _____ , you are involved in a really long race.
10 When you _____ , you do something faster or better than anyone else.
11 When you _____ , you decide something you want to do in the future.
12 When you _____ , you are able to understand funny things and to be funny yourself.

C   **Imagine you are in these situations. What might you say? Use the phrases from exercise 1A to write a sentence for each.**

1   **at a party:**   *Miranda, tell us a good joke.* _____
2   **at a job interview:**   _____
3   **at a sporting event:**   _____

2 GRAMMAR: Tense review (simple and continuous)

A **Some of the underlined verbs are not correct. Fix the mistakes.**

1 I <u>~~was going~~</u> *went* to a party last night. It <u>was</u> fun.

2 What <u>do</u> you <u>do</u> right now? <u>Are</u> you busy?

3 Jorge <u>has gotten</u> a job, but Rosa <u>has looked</u> for six months and <u>is</u> still <u>looking</u>.

4 <u>Have</u> you <u>heard</u> the news? Tony and Ana <u>have been getting</u> married.

5 I <u>talked</u> to Julia when you <u>called</u>. She <u>was telling</u> me a funny story.

B **Complete the paragraph with the correct form of the verbs in the box. Some verbs will be used more than once.**

~~be~~	get	(not) see	take	talk	wait	walk

There ¹_____ *have been* _____ strange events in my neighborhood recently. I ²_____ down the street a couple of days ago when I ³_____ a cow. Yes, that's right, a cow! You ⁴_____ often _____ cows in the middle of a city. In fact, I ⁵_____ never _____ one. But last Monday at 4:15 in the afternoon, there ⁶_____ a cow in the middle of the road. Drivers ⁷_____ out of their cars. A lot of people ⁸_____ pictures. People in the neighborhood ⁹_____ to each other about the cow ever since. We ¹⁰_____ to see what the next strange event will be.

C **Write true sentences about you. Replace X with a word or phrase to complete each sentence.**

1 In my entire life, I / never / see / X

   In my entire life, I've never seen a cow on a street. _____

2 I / walk / down the street the other day when / X

   _____

3 You / often / (not) see / X / in my neighborhood

   _____

4 Once / I / X / but / I / never / X / it again

   _____

5 I / X / right now because I / X

   _____

6 I / try to / X / for a long time / but / I / still / X

   _____

1.2 THE RIGHT CANDIDATE

1 VOCABULARY: Describing key qualities

A **Check (✓) the correct underlined words. Correct the incorrect words.**

1 He is a very ~~responsibility~~ *responsible* person. ☐
2 She has the right <u>qualifications</u> for the job. ☑
3 He has a lot of <u>curious</u>. ☐
4 I hope to be very <u>success</u> in the future. ☐
5 I like their <u>independence</u>. ☐
6 You're not very <u>ambitious</u>, are you? ☐
7 I'm very <u>experience</u>. ☐
8 It's important to treat people <u>polite</u>. ☐
9 This job requires a lot of <u>creativity</u>. ☐
10 She doesn't have much <u>enthusiastic</u>. ☐
11 Thank you for your <u>truthfulness</u>. ☐
12 Are you <u>confident</u> when you speak English? ☐

2 GRAMMAR: Stative and dynamic verbs

A **Write *S* (stative verb) or *D* (dynamic verb).**

1 Are you being truthful?   D
2 We usually interview five people for every job. _____
3 I take a photography class on Tuesday evenings. _____
4 The report is very interesting. _____
5 Do you know Lily? _____
6 Why do they hate their job? _____
7 I need some help. _____
8 I'm thinking of changing jobs. _____

B **Complete each pair of sentences with the stative and dynamic use of the verb in parentheses ( ).**

1 (see)
   a Tom _____is seeing_____ the doctor. He'll be home soon.
   b I _____see_____ two people outside.

2 (have)
   a Melina _____ experience.
   b The doctor's in the cafeteria. She _____ lunch.

3 (think)
   a We _____ about moving to a bigger place.
   b What _____ you _____ of the class?

4 (smell)
   a He _____ the fish. Maybe there's something wrong with it.
   b Everything _____ delicious. Let's eat!

5 (weigh)
   a The suitcase _____ 22 kilos.
   b I don't know the price yet. The man _____ the meat now.

3 GRAMMAR AND VOCABULARY

A **Complete the job reference for Alex Martinez. Use the correct form of the verbs in parentheses ( ). What qualities from exercise 1A does he have? Circle them.**

I [1] _____know_____ (know) Alex well. I [2] _____ (know) him for ten years. He [3] _____ (work) at the company for six. He is a (responsible) person and [4] _____ (take) his job very seriously. He is definitely qualified for the job. He [5] _____ (have) two degrees and many years of experience. He's ambitious and clearly [6] _____ (want) to be successful. He [7] _____ (set) goals for himself and then [8] _____ (do) the work to achieve them. He is curious and loves to learn new things. He [9] _____ (talk) to a lot of people who are different from him and [10] _____ (try) to learn from them. In fact, right now he [11] _____ (take) two classes at the local community college in different subjects. I'm not surprised that Alex [12] _____ (look) for a job with more responsibilities. His confidence is just another one of his excellent qualities. We will be sorry to lose him.

B **Use the word prompts to write part of a job reference for someone you know. Replace X with a word or phrase to complete each sentence.**

1 She/He / work / at this job / X years
   She has worked at this job for three years.

2 She/He / X / worker
   _____
   _____

3 Right now / she/he / X
   _____
   _____

4 Her/His / X / one of her/his excellent qualities
   _____
   _____

1.3 WE GO WAY BACK

1 FUNCTIONAL LANGUAGE: Making and responding to introductions

A **Complete the sentences. Match 1–7 in column A with a–g in column B.**

A		B	
1 Do you …	_c_	**a**	here, right?
2 I don't think …		**b**	met my assistant?
3 You're new …		**c**	know anyone here?
4 Do you two know …		**d**	first day?
5 Have you …		**e**	to a couple of people.
6 Let me introduce you …		**f**	we've met before.
7 Is this your …		**g**	each other?

B **Put the conversation in the correct order.**

Jack	Yes, I just started this morning.	____
Jack	It's nice to meet you, Sofia.	____
Sofia	Hello. I don't think we've met before.	_1_
Sofia	My name is Sofia.	____
Sofia	It's nice to meet you, too. Is this your first day?	____
Jack	No, we haven't met yet. I'm Jack.	____

2 REAL-WORLD STRATEGY: Responding to an introduction

A **Complete the conversations. Use the words in the box.**

go	going	haven't	hi	I'm	love	met	see	~~sure~~	went

1 Dan Have you met Sandra?

   Luis I'm not _____sure_____, but _____, I'm Luis.

2 Dan Do you know Sandra?

   Chris Yes, we _____ way back. We _____ to school together. How's it _____, Sandra?

3 Dan Have you met Sandra?

   Marta No, I _____, but I'd _____ to. Hi, Sandra. _____ Marta.

4 Dan Do you two know each other?

   Ruta Yes, we _____ this morning! Nice to _____ you again, Sandra.

3 FUNCTIONAL LANGUAGE AND REAL-WORLD STRATEGY

A **Complete the conversation. Use the language you practiced in exercises 1A and 2A.**

1 **Armando** Hi. I don't think we've met before.
_____ *You're new* _____ here, right?

Clara _____ yesterday

Armando I'm Armando.

Clara Nice _____ . I'm Clara.

Armando Nice to meet you, too, Clara. Let me
_____ . Tom, this is Clara.

Tom Hey Clara! _____ ?

Armando _____ each other?

Clara Yeah, _____ yesterday.

2 **Sara** Is this your _____ ?
I'm Sara.

Rick Hi Sara. It's _____ .
I'm Rick.

Sara Do you _____ ?

Rick No, not yet.

Sara _____
to a couple of people. Zack, this is Rick.

Zack _____ , Rick.

Rick _____ , too.

B **Choose one of the following situations. Write a conversation introducing the people. Use the language you practiced in exercises 1 A and 2A.**

Situation 1: Marcel has just moved into your neighborhood. Introduce yourself.

Situation 2: Francesca is new to your class. Introduce her to some of your classmates.

A _____

_____

B _____

_____

A _____

_____

B _____

_____

FLIPPING YOUR JOB INTERVIEW

1 READING

A **Read the blog post. Then check (✓) the best title.**

1 Preparing for an interview? ☐

2 Getting the job you want! ☐

3 Dress for success! ☐

●●● ⟨ ⟩ 🔍 🏠

| Blog | Share | Comment |

You've finally gotten the interview you've wanted for months. Now you're busy preparing for the interview. You've researched the company and thought about the questions you want to ask.

What else is there? What you're going to wear. The way you look is very important. At the end of the interview, you want people to be talking about your experience, not your appearance.

What should you wear? Suits and ties for guys, and dresses for women? That's not always necessary. It depends on the type of job you're applying for.

Is it a job in the computer industry? You might not need a suit or a dress, but that doesn't mean you can go in a T-shirt and jeans. You need to look like you're going to work, not out for the night with friends. So, guys, put on a nice shirt and stylish pants. And, women, a nice sweater or blouse with a skirt or pants will be fine.

If you're interviewing for a finance job, you need to wear what people in the business world wear. That means a suit and tie for men and dresses or suits for women.

Dress for the job you want. Make sure your clothes are clean and ironed. Avoid wearing perfume or cologne, and don't wear too much makeup or jewelry.

Remember: If after the interview people are talking about your appearance, you probably won't hear from them again. So dress right and look good. Your career may depend on it.

B **READ FOR GIST** **Complete the statements. Use the phrases in the box.**

goes to a lot of job interviews	has interviewed people	buy clothes
is going to go to a job interview	get a job	interview people

1 The person who wrote the article is someone who _____.

2 The person who reads the article is someone who _____.

3 The purpose of the article is to help someone _____.

2 LISTENING

A 🔊 **1.01** **Listen to the conversation. Answer the questions.**

1 When is the man's interview? _____

2 Where has he applied for a job? _____

3 What should he wear? _____

4 What's the problem? _____

3 WRITING

A Read the comments in response to the blog post in exercise 1A. Underline the sentence that shows agreement. Circle the sentence that shows disagreement. Put a box around the sentences that show appreciation.

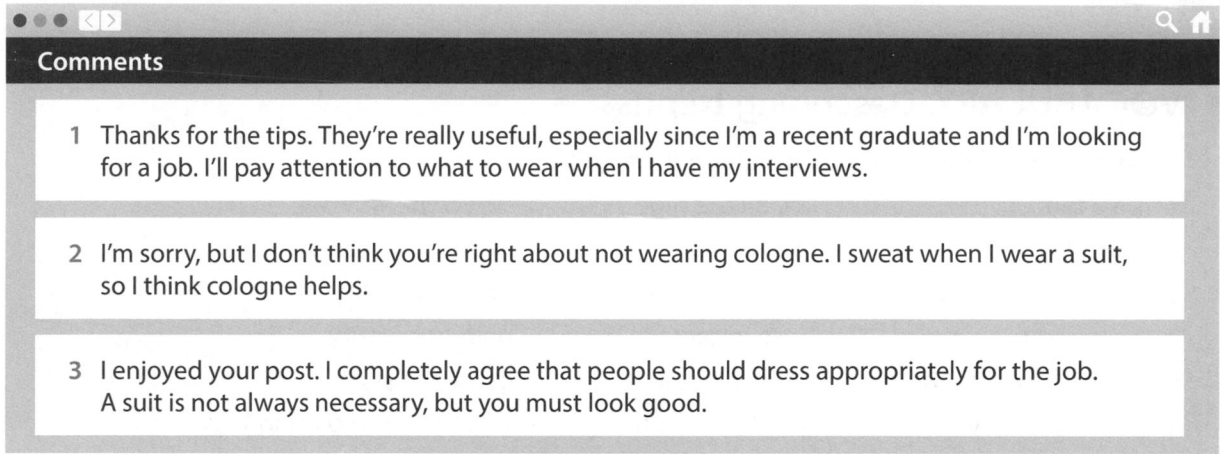

Comments

1 Thanks for the tips. They're really useful, especially since I'm a recent graduate and I'm looking for a job. I'll pay attention to what to wear when I have my interviews.

2 I'm sorry, but I don't think you're right about not wearing cologne. I sweat when I wear a suit, so I think cologne helps.

3 I enjoyed your post. I completely agree that people should dress appropriately for the job. A suit is not always necessary, but you must look good.

B Write two comments in response to the blog post in exercise 1A. In one comment, show appreciation and agree. In the second comment, disagree. Which comment reflects your true opinion?

CHECK AND REVIEW

Read the statements. Can you do these things?

UNIT 1	Mark the boxes. ☑ I can do it. ? I am not sure. I can ...	If you are not sure, go back to these pages in the Student's Book.
VOCABULARY	☐ use expressions to talk about personal achievements.	page 2
	☐ use nouns and adjectives to talk about key qualities employers look for.	page 4
GRAMMAR	☐ use a variety of simple and continuous verb forms.	page 3
	☐ use dynamic and stative verbs to talk about actions, habits, and states.	page 5
FUNCTIONAL LANGUAGE	☐ make introductions.	page 6
	☐ respond to an introduction.	page 7
SKILLS	☐ write a comment in response to a blog post.	page 9
	☐ agree, disagree, and show appreciation.	page 9

UNIT 2 THE FUTURE OF FOOD

2.1 MENU WITH A MISSION

1 VOCABULARY: Describing trends

A **Cross out the phrase that is different in meaning.**

1	be a fad	be all the rage	~~be on the way out~~
2	be dated	be fashionable	be old-fashioned
3	come back in style	go out of fashion	lose popularity
4	be trendy	lose interest	gain popularity
5	be the next big thing	gain interest	go out of style
6	be on the way out	be the latest thing	be the next big thing

B **Answer the questions about trends.**

1 What is something you think is a fad?

In my opinion, long beards are a fad. I don't think they'll be popular next year.

2 What is a type of clothing you think is dated?

3 What is a type of music that is gaining popularity?

4 What is a type of music that is going out of style?

5 What type of diets are trendy right now?

6 What do you think will be the next big thing in fashion?

7 What is something that is all the rage right now?

8 What is something you think is old-fashioned?

A **Put the words in the correct order to make sentences.**

1 the server / to waste / want / for a doggy bag / ask / don't / you / the food / if

<u>If you don't want to waste the food, ask the server for a doggy bag. OR Ask the server for a doggy bag if you don't want to waste the food.</u>

2 people won't / just a fad / for very long / if / do / it's / it

3 the chocolate pizza / like / if / have / you / to try / different kinds of food / you

4 to waste food / if / get worse / the problem / continue / will / we

5 on social media / everyone / something / trending / pays attention / if / is

6 expensive / a restaurant / if / it / gourmet food / usually / is / serves

B **Complete the sentences. Use the words in parentheses ( ).**

1 Fish _____is_____ (be) good for you if it _____isn't_____ (not / be) fried.

2 If we _____ (not / put) the meat in the fridge soon, it _____ (go) bad.

3 If you _____ (be) allergic to nuts, _____ (not / eat) the cake. It has nuts.

4 _____ (not / drink) coffee at night if you _____ (have) trouble falling asleep.

5 If you _____ (make) dinner tomorrow, I _____ (cook) it tonight.

6 _____ (not / go) to Heaven Gourmet if you _____ (want) a cheap meal. It's an expensive place.

C **How can people waste less food, eat better, and save money? Write your ideas. Use *if*.**

<u>If you don't eat a lot of fast food, you'll have a healthier diet.</u>

2.2 FOOD YOU FERMENT

1 VOCABULARY: Preparing food

A **Cross out the food that is in a different food group.**

1 ~~pineapple~~   garlic   mint
2 eggplant   tuna   zucchini
3 garlic   shrimp   tuna
4 cabbage   pineapple   zucchini
5 ginger   mint   zucchini

B **Complete the sentences with words from exercise 1A. More than one answer may be possible.**

1 Mariel likes to put a little bit of _____ in her tea.

2 Do you have a stick of gum or a breath mint? The pasta I had for lunch had too much _____ in it.

3 Jack went fishing last weekend and caught a 40-lb _____!

4 I have to remove the shells from these _____ before we cook them. Can you help me?

5 _____ is probably my favorite vegetable. I just love its purple color.

C **Complete the sentences. Use the words in the box.**

~~barbecue~~	boil	chop	fry	rinse	stir

1 If you ____barbecue____ a steak, you usually do it outside.
2 If you _____ fruit, you usually do it at the sink.
3 You need a spoon to _____ something.
4 If you _____ water, it becomes very hot.
5 You need a knife to _____ something.
6 You need oil to _____ something.

D **Answer the questions with your own information.**

1 Which foods in exercise 1A do you like?

_____

2 Are there foods in exercise 1A you have never tried?

_____

3 How often do you use the cooking methods in exercise 1C?

_____

4 What dish do you eat that uses a food from exercise 1A and a cooking method from exercise 1C?

_____

2 GRAMMAR: Clauses with *when, until, after*

A **Underline the event in each sentence that happens first.**

1 The sauce will change color when <u>you add the garlic</u>.
2 As soon as the food is done, we'll eat.
3 Before the water boils, put in the cabbage.
4 Add the zucchini after you fry the fish.
5 Cook the rice until there's no more water in the pot.
6 Once we finish lunch, we'll wash the dishes.

B **Combine the sentences. Use the time expression in parentheses ( ).**

1 I'm going to reserve a table. Then I'll tell you the time. (after)

<u>After I reserve a table, I'll tell you the time. OR I'll tell you the time after I reserve a table.</u>

2 We'll get to the restaurant. Then we'll text you. (when)

_____

3 We'll wait outside. You will arrive. (until)

_____

4 The server will give us the menu. We'll order. (as soon as)

_____

5 We'll pay the bill. Then we'll leave. (once)

_____

6 We'll have dinner. Then we'll go to the movies. (before)

_____

C **Write the correct form of the verb in parentheses ( ).**
Then complete the sentence with your own information.

1 When I _____cook_____ (cook) a big meal, _____I'll invite all my friends_____ .
2 After I _____ (get up) tomorrow morning, _____ .
3 I _____ (not go) to bed until _____ .
4 As soon as I _____ (have) some free time, _____ .
5 Once I _____ (save) enough money, _____ .

2.3 CAN I GET YOU A REFILL?

1 FUNCTIONAL LANGUAGE: Make, accept, and refuse offers

A Change the underlined words in the sentences without changing the meaning. Use the words in the box.

| I'm OK | a refill | care for | get | here |
| Awesome | offer | Oh | wonderful | want |

1 **A** Can I get you <s>another juice</s>? *a refill*

   B <u>I'd better not</u>, thanks.

2 **A** Would you <u>like</u> some juice?

   B That'd be <u>great</u>.

3 **A** Can I <u>get</u> you another dessert?

   B <u>Yes</u>, that's great.

4 **A** Can I <u>have</u> another sausage, please?

   B Sure, <u>there</u> you go.

5 **A** Anyone else <u>care for</u> some cake? We have three different kinds.

   B <u>That's great</u>, I'll check it out.

2 REAL-WORLD STRATEGY: Acknowledge an acceptance

A Read each conversation. Use the words below to complete each response.

| back | got | right | sure |

1 **A** Can I offer you anything to drink?

   B Yes. Some coffee would be great.

   A I'll be right _____ with that.

2 **A** Would you pass me another cookie, please?

   B _____ thing.

3 **A** Is there any more iced tea?

   B Coming _____ up!

4 **A** Could I have a little more cake? It's delicious.

   B You _____ it!

B Write two conversations. Speaker A makes an offer of food or drink. Speaker B accepts or refuses.

1 **A** _____

   B _____

   A _____

2 **A** _____

   B _____

   A _____

3 FUNCTIONAL LANGUAGE AND REAL-WORLD STRATEGY

A **What do people often offer in these situations? Write three things.**

On an airplane	At a party	At a business meeting	At a restaurant
something to drink			
a snack			
a blanket			

B **Write conversations for each remaining situation in exercise 3A. Have people accept and refuse the offers.**

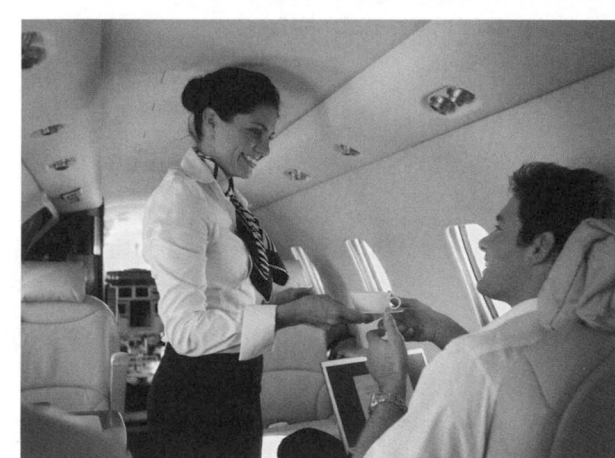

Flight attendant	Would you like something to drink?
Passenger	Yes, I'd love a glass of water.
Flight attendant	Coming right up!
Flight attendant	Can I get you a snack?
Passenger	I'd better not, thanks.
Flight attendant	Would you care for a blanket?
Passenger	That'd be wonderful.

Conversation 1

A _____

B _____

A _____

B _____

A _____

B _____

A _____

Conversation 2

A _____

B _____

A _____

B _____

A _____

B _____

A _____

Conversation 3

A _____

B _____

A _____

B _____

A _____

B _____

A _____

2.4 COOL FOOD

1 LISTENING

A 🔊 **2.01** **LISTEN FOR GIST** **Listen to a conversation between a man and a woman. Where do they decide to have lunch? Why?**

B 🔊 **2.01** **Listen again. Read the statements. Write *T* (true) or *F* (false). Correct the statements that are false.**

1 The woman is on a gluten-free diet because she wants to lose weight. _____

2 The woman has avoided eating things with gluten for the past six months. _____

3 The woman's family is also on a gluten-free diet. _____

4 The man and the woman are definitely going to lunch at Anna's. _____

2 READING

A **Read about the results of a survey about gluten-free diets. Circle the questions that the survey asked. Answer the questions you circle.**

> Gluten-free diets seem all the rage nowadays. You can see gluten-free foods in supermarkets and restaurants. News about the gluten-free diets of movie stars and professional athletes is all over social media. But what do people really know about gluten-free foods? Our survey results have some surprises.
>
> A majority of the people who responded said that being on a gluten-free diet improves physical or mental health. About 22 percent said they buy gluten-free products or try to avoid gluten.
>
> A quarter of the people in the survey thought that gluten-free foods have more nutrients than food with gluten. The truth is just the opposite.
>
> More than a third of the people interviewed thought that a gluten-free diet will help them lose weight. However, there is no research that proves this to be true. In fact, studies have shown that gluten-free diets can increase the risk of becoming overweight.

1 Does being on a gluten-free diet improve physical or mental health?

2 Do you buy gluten-free products or try to avoid gluten?

3 Is gluten-free food less expensive?

4 Do gluten-free foods have more nutrients than food with gluten?

5 Will a gluten-free diet help you lose weight?

3 WRITING

A Look at the charts from a college survey on what students drink. What trends do they show?

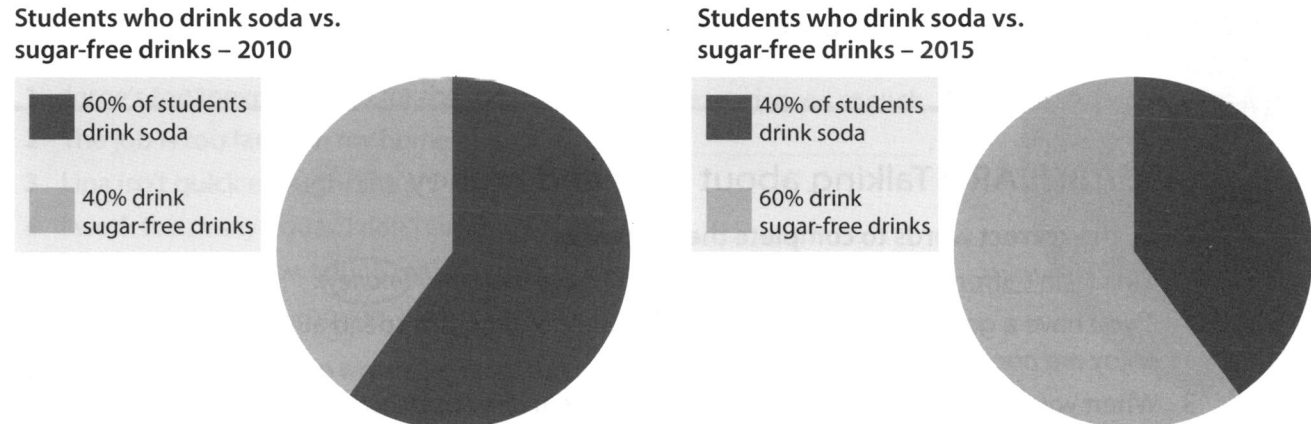

Students who drink soda vs.
sugar-free drinks – 2010

- 60% of students drink soda
- 40% drink sugar-free drinks

Students who drink soda vs.
sugar-free drinks – 2015

- 40% of students drink soda
- 60% drink sugar-free drinks

B Write a short report about the survey results. You can use the phrases below. Make sure you include numbers from the chart.

> gain/lose popularity   be trendy   be on the way out   be a thing of the past
> be the next big thing

CHECK AND REVIEW

Read the statements. Can you do these things?

UNIT 2	Mark the boxes. ☑ I can do it. ? I am not sure. I can ...	If you are not sure, go back to these pages in the Student's Book.
VOCABULARY	☐ use expressions to describe trends. ☐ use the correct words to describe food preparation.	page 12 page 14
GRAMMAR	☐ use real conditionals. ☐ refer to the future with time clauses using *when*, *until*, and *after*.	page 13 page 15
FUNCTIONAL LANGUAGE	☐ make, accept, and refuse offers. ☐ acknowledge an acceptance	page 16 page 17
SKILLS	☐ write survey results. ☐ reference numbers and statistics.	page 19 page 19

3.3 I'M SO SORRY!

1 FUNCTIONAL LANGUAGE: Apologize for damaging something

A Complete the conversation. Use the words in the box.

can't	didn't	don't	dumbest	how	so	~~sorry~~	what

Martin I'm really ¹_____sorry_____ , but I just did the ²_____ thing.

Althea Oh no, ³_____ tell me something happened to my car. Did someone steal it?

Martin No, no. The car's outside. It's just that I had a small accident. You'll never guess ⁴_____ I did.

Althea What happened?

Martin I was parking the car and hit a tree. I can't tell you ⁵_____ sorry I am.

Althea A tree?

Martin I know. I ⁶_____ believe I ⁷_____ see it. I am ⁸_____ sorry. I'll pay for the damage.

Althea Let me call the insurance company and see if they'll pay. But first, let me see the car.

2 REAL-WORLD STRATEGY: Responding to an apology

A Respond to the apologies. Put the words in the correct order.

1 Glen I'm so sorry I was late for the meeting.

　Andy deal / it's / big / really / no

　_____

　_____

2 Delcy I can't believe I forgot your birthday.

　Nate over / don't / yourself / it / beat / up

　_____

　_____

3 Ron I'm really sorry I didn't pick you up on time.

　Hee-an end / the / the / not / world / it's / of

　_____

　_____

3 FUNCTIONAL LANGUAGE AND REAL-WORLD STRATEGY

A **Write a conversation for each situation. Use the language you practiced in exercises 1A and 2A.**

1 Victor lost Daria's book. He left it on the train. Daria doesn't want him to feel bad about it.

Victor Daria, I can't believe I did this but …

Daria Oh no, what?

Victor I left your book on the train. I can't tell you how sorry I am.

Daria It's just a book. Don't beat yourself up over it.

2 Keiko forgot about a meeting. She didn't put it on her calendar. Al doesn't want her to feel bad about it.

Keiko _____

Al _____

Keiko _____

Al _____

3 Joao texted Max the wrong directions, and Max got lost. Max doesn't want him to feel bad about it.

Joao _____

Max _____

Joao _____

Max _____

4 Alex is out of town. His friend Lin is staying at his apartment. Lin calls Alex to tell him something has happened and to apologize. Alex thinks Lin is going to tell him he broke the TV.

Lin _____

Alex _____

Lin _____

Alex _____

5 Hector says he broke one of Alice's good glasses. Alice doesn't want him to feel bad about it.

Hector _____

Alice _____

Hector _____

Alice _____

EPIC SHOPPING FAILS

1 READING

A **Read the blog post about shopping. Is the blogger writing about shopping online or in a store?**

● ● ● ◁ ▷   🔍 🏠

| Blog | Comment | Like | Share |

I'm doing my best not to shop online because I want to help local businesses. Too many of them are closing. If we don't shop in stores, there won't be any in a few years. But stores, you're going to have to make some changes if you want customers to keep coming. What happened to me yesterday tells you why.

I went to a local electronics store. I got to the parking lot. It was huge, but I drove around for 10 minutes until I could find a space. So I was already annoyed before I even entered the store.

Anyway, I was finally in the store. Right away a salesperson started following me. That was really annoying. He only left when another customer asked for something. A few minutes later when I wanted some information about a product, I couldn't find anyone to help me. I wandered around for 5 minutes until I finally found someone, and he didn't have enough information about the product to help me!

Your customers' time is valuable. We don't want to wait for anything – not to park, not to get information, and definitely not to pay. (One cash register for five customers? I waited 15 minutes to pay. That was way too long.) I'm willing to pay a fair price for your product, but you have to make it worth it for me to shop at your store. If not, there's always online!

B **READ FOR DETAIL** **Read the post again. Answer the questions.**

1 What does the blogger say about the parking lot?

   a It was too small.   **b** It was too full.

2 Why wasn't the salesperson helpful?

   a He didn't know about the product.   **b** He was rude.

3 What other problem did the blogger have?

   a She had to wait too long to pay.   **b** The store didn't have the product she wanted.

2 LISTENING

A 🔊 **3.01** **Listen to the conversation. Answer the questions.**

1 What kind of business does the woman work at? _____

2 Who gives her problems at work? _____

3 What did the Milk Lady do? _____

4 Why can't the woman fix the problem? _____

A   **Read the store review. Underline the sentence that shows the reviewer's feeling. Circle the positive and negative features of the store. Put a box around the sentence that gives a recommendation.**

> ● ● ● ◁ ▷   🔍 🏠
>
> **Store review**
>
> I highly recommend ProSports. I recently bought a tennis racket there. It's an excellent store with a wide variety of products and great prices. I couldn't find anything cheaper online. My only complaint is that there wasn't enough staff. Everyone was very friendly and knew a lot about the products, but there wasn't enough staff to take care of all the customers. Maybe that was because too many people know that ProSports is such a great store. It was my first time there. I'd definitely go back.

B   **Think of a store you have been to recently. Write a short review of the store.**

_____

_____

_____

_____

_____

_____

_____

_____

CHECK AND REVIEW

Read the statements. Can you do these things?

UNIT 3	Mark the boxes. ☑ I can do it. ? I am not sure.		If you are not sure, go back to these pages in the Student's Book.
	I can …		
VOCABULARY	☐ **use expressions to talk about time and money.**		page 22
	☐ **use verb phrases to talk about prices and value.**		page 24
GRAMMAR	☐ **use (*not*) *too* and (*not*) *enough* to talk about quantity.**		page 23
	☐ **use modifiers in comparisons.**		page 25
FUNCTIONAL LANGUAGE	☐ **apologize for damaging something.**		page 26
	☐ **respond to an apology.**		page 27
SKILLS	☐ **write a product review.**		page 29
	☐ **describe feelings and give recommendations.**		page 29

1 VOCABULARY: Talking about advertising

A Complete the sentences with words in the box.

advertise	ad/advertisement	brands	commercials	fashion statement
logo	merchandise	merchandising	products	slogan
~~sponsor (n.)~~	sponsor (v.)	status symbols		

1 Al's Pizza pays to support our basketball team. They are our _____sponsor_____ . We have their _____ – "Best pizza in town!" – on our jerseys.

2 Louisa wears bright colors to make a _____ .

3 Dave's business was not doing well, so he decided to _____ on TV. He also hired an artist to design a new _____ for his business.

4 Have you seen the _____ for that new TV show? It looks really funny.

5 _____ from famous _____ , like Gucci and Prada, are often more expensive because they are _____ .

6 Disney makes a lot of its profits from _____ . The company charges other companies to put its characters on their products.

7 Many websites make money by hosting _____ for other companies and products.

8 Many companies will _____ a local charity or a sports team because they know it is good for their reputation.

9 The football stadium has a store inside that sells the team's _____ .

2 GRAMMAR: Modals of speculation

A Circle the correct words.

1 The fans are going to their seats. They *can't* / (*must*) have tickets.

2 Val was in second place in the race last time. She *might* / *must* win this time.

3 Andreas always wears a Santos jersey. He *could* / *must* like the team.

4 There's a man talking to the players. He *must* / *could* be the coach. Or maybe he's the referee.

5 Some fans are leaving the game early. They *can't* / *might* be bored.

6 Nobody is wearing a jacket. It *can't* / *could* be cold.

B **Complete the paragraph below. Use the past perfect form of the words in the box.**

be ~~break~~ open put take throw

Julio and Marcella came home late from a party one evening. They were shocked to see that one of the living room windows was broken. Someone ¹_____had broken_____ the glass. The back door was unlocked. Someone ²_____ the door. The dog was in the basement. Someone ³_____ the dog there. They found their books and important papers on the floor. Someone ⁴_____ them off the desk. Their laptops were gone. Someone ⁵_____ them. Julio and Marcella called the police because they ⁶_____ robbed.

3 GRAMMAR AND VOCABULARY

A **Read the story below. Put the events in the correct order. Then decide: Is it a personal tragedy, a feel-good story, or a family saga?**

_____ His parents are very worried.

__1__ A young boy goes fishing with his dog.

_____ The boy is missing for 12 hours.

_____ After a few hours, the boy gets lost.

_____ The parents are very happy.

_____ Luckily, the dog helps him find his way home again.

B **Complete the story from exercise 3A. Use the simple past, past continuous, and past perfect.**

A young boy had gone fishing with his dog. After a few hours,

_____

_____

_____

_____

_____

_____

_____

_____

LAST-MINUTE-ITIS

1 VOCABULARY: Making and breaking plans

A **Complete the phrasal verbs with *ahead, down, out, forward,* or *together*.**

Jess Hi, Leo. What happened last night? We all got ¹_____together_____ at the new pizza place in town. We thought you were coming but then we gave ²_____ on you.

Leo Yeah, I know. Sorry I let you ³_____ . I don't mean to make ⁴_____ excuses, but yesterday was just the worst day. First, my car was stolen. I ended ⁵_____ taking three buses to Gina's place. Then she split ⁶_____ with me.

Jess Really? I'm so sorry. That's terrible. A day like that could mess ⁷_____ your whole month.

Leo Thanks Jess. Right now I'm just trying to stay positive. Anyway, I'm headed to lunch now. Should I wait for you or go ⁸_____ without you?

Jess Don't wait. I'm going to be held ⁹_____ here a little longer. Do you want to do something later today, maybe to cheer you ¹⁰_____ ?

Leo Thanks, but tonight I'm going to hang ¹¹_____ with my family. And I also feel like I'm getting a cold.

Jess Well, I'm sure you're looking ¹²_____ to your vacation at least. Vacations always make me feel better.

Leo Definitely. After all this it will be nice to get away for a couple of days. But let's get ¹³_____ when I'm back.

2 GRAMMAR: *was/were going to; was/were supposed to*

A **Check (✓) the correct sentences.**

1 I was going call you, but I forgot. ☐

2 We were going to leave at 8, but we left at 9. ☑

3 The kids were suppose to get out of school an hour ago. Where are they? ☐

4 You going to pay me last week. I'm still waiting for the money. ☐

5 It supposed to rain today, but it's a beautiful day. ☐

6 Was I supposed to meet Professor Yu yesterday? I can't remember. ☐

B **Now correct the incorrect sentences from exercise 2A.**

I was going to call you, but I forgot.

_____

_____

_____

_____

_____

C Manuel checked the things he did last week. Complete the sentences about the things he did <u>not</u> do. Use *was/were going to* in 1–3 and *was/were supposed to* in 4–6.

Reminders
buy a new jacket
play tennis with Sam
sign up for an art class
get my car fixed ✓
meet Ali for dinner
see Dr. Garcia ✓
send a gift to Rena
visit Aunt Rita

1 _He was going to buy a new jacket_ , but he didn't.
2 _____ , but he didn't.
3 _____ , but he didn't.
4 _____ , but he didn't.
5 _____ , but he didn't.
6 _____ , but he didn't.

3 GRAMMAR AND VOCABULARY

A Complete the sentences. Use the words in parentheses ( ) and the correct form of the phrasal verbs in the box.

| cheer up | get together | go ahead | ~~hang out~~ |
| make up | mess up | split up | |

1 Luis and his friends _____were going to hang out_____ (going to) at the mall last night, but the mall closed early.

2 I _____ (going to) with my friends for a movie, but I was held up.

3 The band _____ (going to) after their June concert, but they played together for one more year.

4 Charlie wasn't feeling well, but his parents _____ (going to) with the party. Then they changed their minds.

5 The party _____ (supposed to) Elisa, but it didn't. She was still sad.

6 Jessica _____ (going to) an excuse for missing the test. But in the end she told the truth.

7 Updating the operating system _____ (not supposed to) my phone, but it sure did. It won't even turn on now!

5.3 THERE MUST BE A MISTAKE!

1 FUNCTIONAL LANGUAGE: Reacting to bad news

A **Read the reactions to a problem. Circle the correct words. Then label each sentence _reaction,_ _escalation,_ or _resolution._**

1 _There is / (Is there)_ someone _(else) / more_ I can speak to about this, please?   _escalation_

2 I _'m not / don't_ get it.

3 I'm just glad _that / that's_ settled.

4 _You can / Can you_ check again, please?

5 _That's / This is_ quite all right.

6 _Will / Would_ you mind _take / taking_ another look?

7 I don't _get / understand._

8 There _can / must_ be something you _can / must_ do.

9 There _might / must_ be _a / some_ kind of mistake.

10 I _like / 'd like_ to speak to _manager / the manager,_ please.

2 REAL-WORLD STRATEGY: Accepting bad news

A **Put the words in order to complete the responses.**

1 **Salesperson** I can't lower the price of the car.

You that's not / to hear / but / what / can you / do / I hoped / what

_____ ?

2 **Server** I'm sorry, but there's no more chicken soup today.

You it / it / what / is / well / is

_____ .

3 **Manager** You can't leave work early today.

You life / well / that's

_____ .

4 **Dry cleaner** I'm sorry, but your jacket isn't ready yet.

You too / that's / bad

_____

_____

_____

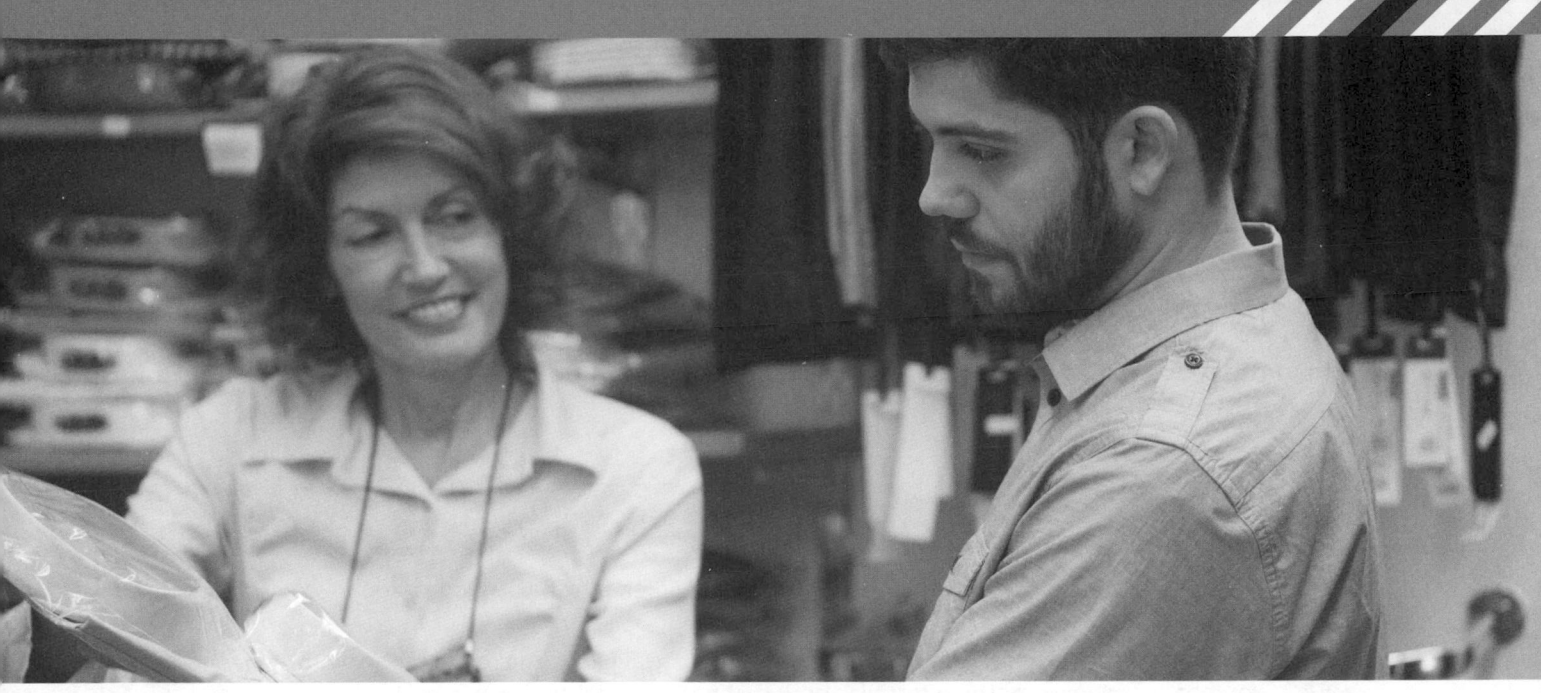

3 FUNCTIONAL LANGUAGE AND REAL-WORLD STRATEGY

A **Jason is in a store and is speaking to Alma at the cash register. Put the sentences in the correct order.**

Alma	The shirt is $50. It's $35 if you pay in cash.	_____
Alma	The sign says $35. Then in small letters it says "Cash."	_____
Jason	Here's my credit card for the shirt. It's $35, right?	1
Jason	There must be some kind of mistake. The sign says $35.	_____
Alma	The manager is busy. How about I give you this $15 tie for only $5?	_____
Jason	That's not right. Is there someone else I can speak to about this, please?	_____
Jason	Well, OK. I've never heard of a credit card difference in price, but I'm glad it's settled. Thanks.	_____

B **Read the situation. Then complete the conversation using the expressions from exercises 1A and 2A.**

Situation: Arturo lost his credit card yesterday. Today he checked online and noticed a lot of new charges on his credit card. He calls the credit card company to ask them to remove the charges and cancel his card.

Credit card worker	Max One credit card. How may I help you?
Arturo	Hi. I lost my credit card yesterday, and today there are some charges on my card that I didn't make. I'd like to have those charges removed and have my credit card canceled.
Credit card worker	Well, I can cancel your credit card, but I can't remove the charges, sir.
Arturo	_____
Credit card worker	I'm sorry sir, but there isn't. You will be responsible for those charges.
Arturo	_____
Credit card worker	Of course, sir. I'll transfer you right now.
Manager	Hello sir. How can I help you?
Arturo	Well, I'm trying to get some charges removed from my credit card account. I lost my card yesterday, and I guess someone else found it and used it.
Manager	I'm sorry to hear that. But since you didn't report your card as lost yesterday, I can't totally remove the charges. But I can reduce them by 50%.
Arturo	_____ .

5.4 THE PERFECT APOLOGY?

1 READING

A **Read the blog post about apologies. Does the writer think apologies matter a little or a lot? How do you know?**

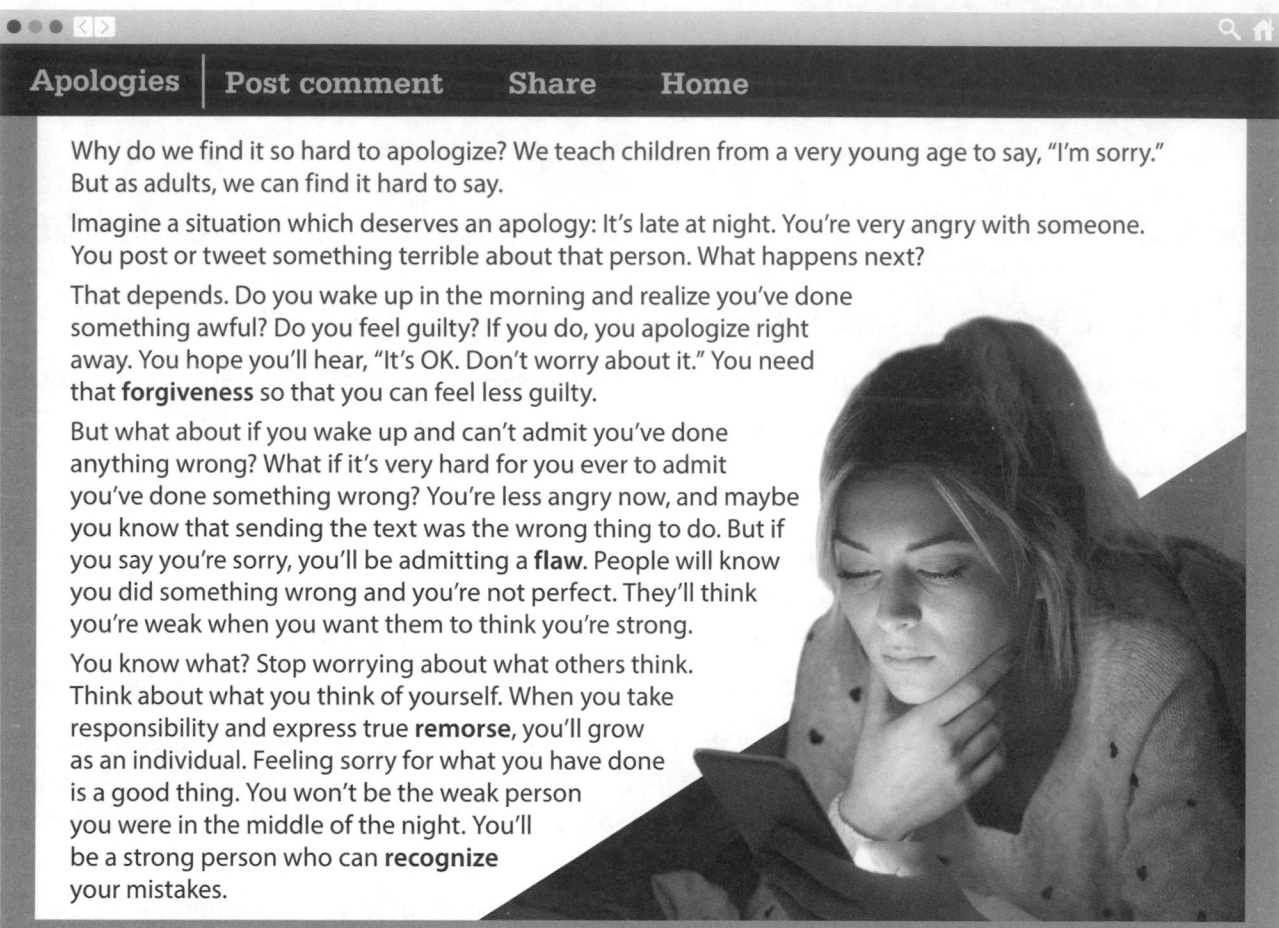

Apologies | **Post comment** **Share** **Home**

Why do we find it so hard to apologize? We teach children from a very young age to say, "I'm sorry." But as adults, we can find it hard to say.

Imagine a situation which deserves an apology: It's late at night. You're very angry with someone. You post or tweet something terrible about that person. What happens next?

That depends. Do you wake up in the morning and realize you've done something awful? Do you feel guilty? If you do, you apologize right away. You hope you'll hear, "It's OK. Don't worry about it." You need that **forgiveness** so that you can feel less guilty.

But what about if you wake up and can't admit you've done anything wrong? What if it's very hard for you ever to admit you've done something wrong? You're less angry now, and maybe you know that sending the text was the wrong thing to do. But if you say you're sorry, you'll be admitting a **flaw**. People will know you did something wrong and you're not perfect. They'll think you're weak when you want them to think you're strong.

You know what? Stop worrying about what others think. Think about what you think of yourself. When you take responsibility and express true **remorse**, you'll grow as an individual. Feeling sorry for what you have done is a good thing. You won't be the weak person you were in the middle of the night. You'll be a strong person who can **recognize** your mistakes.

B **UNDERSTANDING MEANING FROM CONTEXT Match the words from the reading (1–4) with their meaning (a–d). Then underline the words in the text that helped you guess the meaning.**

1 forgiveness _____   a the feeling that you are sorry for something bad you have done

2 flaw _____   b admit that something that is often unpleasant is true

3 remorse _____   c something about us that shows we are not perfect

4 recognize _____   d no longer being angry at someone who has done something bad to you

2 LISTENING

A 🔊 **5.01 Listen to the conversation. Check (✓) the things the man and the woman mention.**

1 The man says what he did wrong. ☐

2 The woman gives advice about making apologies. ☐

3 The woman tells Marco words he should not use in an apology. ☐

4 The man says what happened after he apologized. ☐

3 WRITING

A Read the note of apology. Underline the parts where the writer uses the same language in two different sentences. Then replace the repeated words with words from the box.

offer you this gift   ~~his behavior~~   his service

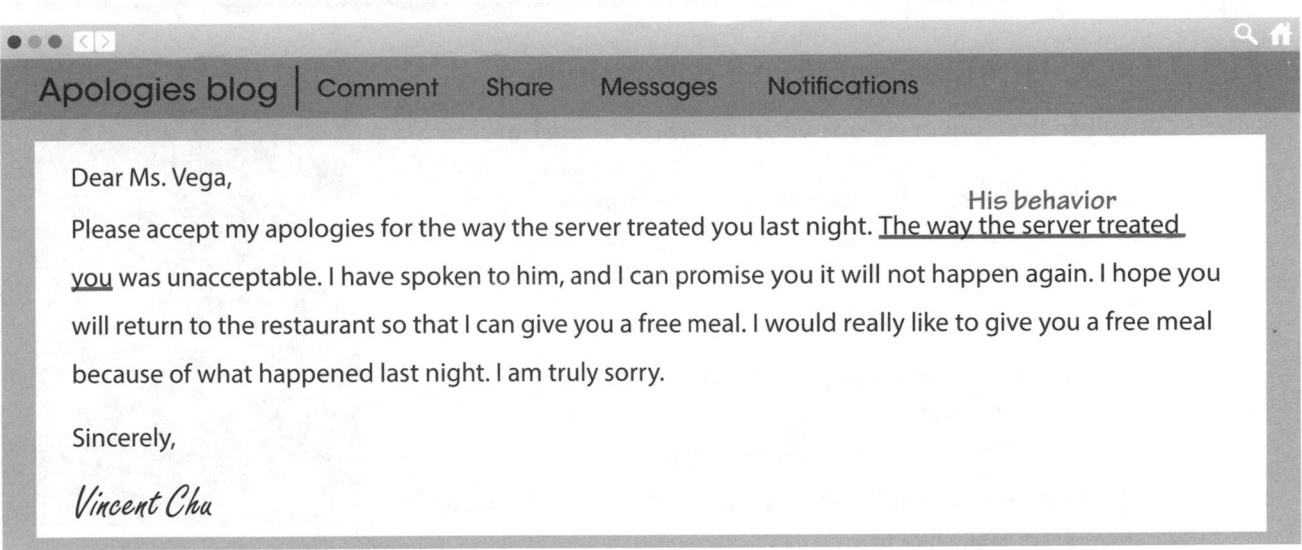

Apologies blog | Comment   Share   Messages   Notifications

Dear Ms. Vega,

His behavior

Please accept my apologies for the way the server treated you last night. <u>The way the server treated you</u> was unacceptable. I have spoken to him, and I can promise you it will not happen again. I hope you will return to the restaurant so that I can give you a free meal. I would really like to give you a free meal because of what happened last night. I am truly sorry.

Sincerely,

Vincent Chu

B You are the owner of a clothing store. Last week, a sales clerk in your store was rude to a customer. Write an apology to the customer. Use the email in exercise 3A as an example.

_____

_____

_____

CHECK AND REVIEW

Read the statements. Can you do these things?

<table>
<tr><td rowspan="11">UNIT 5</td><td colspan="2">Mark the boxes. ☑ I can do it.   ? I am not sure.</td><td rowspan="2">If you are not sure, go back to these pages in the Student's Book.</td></tr>
<tr><td colspan="2">I can …</td></tr>
<tr><td>VOCABULARY</td><td>☐ use specific terms to describe different types of stories.</td><td>page 44</td></tr>
<tr><td></td><td>☐ use expressions to talk about making and breaking plans.</td><td>page 46</td></tr>
<tr><td>GRAMMAR</td><td>☐ order events in the past using the past perfect.</td><td>page 45</td></tr>
<tr><td></td><td>☐ use was/were going to and was/were supposed to for plans in the past that changed or were cancelled.</td><td>page 47</td></tr>
<tr><td>FUNCTIONAL LANGUAGE</td><td>☐ react to problems and disappointing news.</td><td>page 48</td></tr>
<tr><td></td><td>☐ accept bad news.</td><td>page 49</td></tr>
<tr><td>SKILLS</td><td>☐ write an apology.</td><td>page 51</td></tr>
<tr><td></td><td>☐ avoid repetition in writing.</td><td>page 51</td></tr>
</table>

UNIT 6 COMMUNITY ACTION

6.1 HELPING OUT

1 VOCABULARY: Describing communities

A **Complete the conversations with the words in the box.**

bring together	connect with	donate
get involved with	get to know	help out
join	pass on	take care of
~~take part in~~	volunteer	

1 A There's a community garden meeting next week. Would you want to go with me?

 B Yes, I'd like to ___take part in___ that.

2 A Would you like to become a member of our organization?

 B Yes, I'd really like to _____ .

3 A I was wondering if you'd like to give some money to our organization.

 B Sure, I'd be happy to _____ .

4 A Who watches your children when you're at work?

 B My parents _____ them.

5 A Do you have a lot of friends in your new neighborhood?

 B Not really. I need to _____ more people.

6 A I don't get paid for the time I work at the hospital. I do it for free.

 B It's very nice of you to _____ .

7 A My classmates and I have a lot in common.

 B It's good that you have people you can _____ .

8 A Let me carry those boxes for you.

 B It's very kind of you to _____ . Thank you.

9 A Let's have a street party so that all the neighbors can do things with each other.

 B Yes, it will be good to _____ everyone in the neighborhood.

10 A These are the websites that will answer everyone's questions.

 B OK, thanks. I'll _____ the information.

11 A Why did you start to volunteer at the after-school center?

 B I wanted to _____ a group that helps children.

B **Complete the sentences so that they are true for you.**

1 I connect with people by ___talking about sports___ .

2 I've never donated to _____ , but I'd like to.

3 It would be fun to join _____ .

4 I want to get involved with _____ soon.

5 A good way to bring neighbors together is by _____ .

6 It's important to take care of _____ .

GRAMMAR: Present and past passives

A **Underline the object of the sentence. Then rewrite the sentence using the present or past passive tense.**

1 Someone donated <u>millions of dollars</u>.
Millions of dollars were donated.

2 People know the organization all over the world.

3 Someone started the shelter 50 years ago.

4 People give free clothes away every day.

5 Somebody serves the food three times a day.

6 People left their pets on the streets.

B **Complete the sentences with passive verb forms. Use the verbs in parentheses ( ).**

1 I _____ *am given* _____ (give) different things to do every week. That's why I like to volunteer.

2 We _____ (help) right away. It didn't take long for someone to see us.

3 The boys _____ (send) to a different room because they had arrived too late.

4 The students _____ (test) every Monday. They never like it.

5 A doctor _____ (call) when there is an emergency.

6 Our dog _____ (hit) by a car. We were so upset.

C **Write yes/no and information questions. Use the passive. Then look online for the answers.**

1 where / the United Nations / found *Where was the United Nations founded?*
It was founded in San Francisco in the United States.

2 when / the UN building in New York / complete

3 the UN building in New York / design / by a Brazilian architect

4 visitors to the UN building in New York / require / to get a security pass

5 tours of the UN / give / in English only

6.2 RANDOM ACTS OF KINDNESS

1 VOCABULARY: Describing good deeds

A **Circle the correct words.**

1 People should be (grateful) / ungrateful for the kind / (kindness) of others.
2 You can show your *appreciate / appreciation* by saying "thank you."
3 I'm sorry Tom was so *grateful / ungrateful* after all the *helpful / unhelpful* things you did for him.
4 The only *reward / rewarding* I want is your success. That will be very *reward / rewarding*.
5 Sometimes I get advice that is really *helpful / unhelpful*. People say things to me without thinking.
6 I *appreciate / appreciative* everything you have done for me.
7 We were very *appreciate / appreciative* of their *act / action* of kindness.
8 It was very *appreciative / thoughtful* of our neighbors to send food after the fire. I hope we showed our *grateful / gratitude*.
9 When you help someone with something, you are *lending a helping hand / showing your appreciation*.
10 It was a thoughtful gesture to *offer to help repair / think about repairing* the broken window.

B **Answer the questions. Use your own ideas.**

1 How do you show your appreciation for acts of kindness?

2 Who do you like to lend a helping hand to?

3 Why are thoughtful gestures important?

4 What kinds of things are you grateful for?

5 Do you think helping others is its own reward?

6 How do you react if someone is ungrateful for help you offer?

GRAMMAR: Passives with modals

A **Match 1–6 in column A with a–f in column B.**

A

1 Animals here at the zoo should not   _c_
2 Your homework must   _____
3 Donations to the charity can   _____
4 New homes might   _____
5 Thank you so much for everything. Your kindness will   _____
6 Young children should   _____

B

a be remembered.
b be taught to be polite.
c be given any kind of food.
d be found for the homeless.
e be finished by tonight.
f be sent at any time.

B **Complete the sentences using passives with modals. Use the words in parentheses ( ).**

1 Before you help people, they _____ _should be asked_ _____ (should / ask) if they want help.
2 I promise that the report _____ (will / finish) before I leave.
3 This _____ (can't / do) by one person. You need help.
4 Tori _____ (might / give) a job at the animal shelter.
5 I think more money _____ (should / spend) on animals.
6 The boy's injury is serious. He _____ (must / take) to a hospital right away.

C **Answer the questions using passives with modals and the words in parentheses ( ). Then write another answer to the question using passives with modals and your own ideas.**

1 What can happen at home? (food / cook in a microwave oven)

Food can be cooked in a microwave oven.

Clothes can be washed in a washing machine.

2 What must happen at airports? (bags / check)

_____

_____

3 What should happen in parks? (children / watch)

_____

_____

4 What will happen in your next class? (we / give a homework assignment)

_____

_____

5 What might happen in stores? (customers / tell the wrong price)

_____

_____

THERE'S NO NEED …

1 FUNCTIONAL LANGUAGE: Making offers

A **Complete the conversations. Use the words in the box. Write two more conversations using your own ideas.**

anyway	appreciate	can	good
kind	let	like	manage

1 A Would you _____ to sit down?

   B I'm OK. Thanks _____.

2 A _____ I help you with those grocery bags?

   B Thanks, I really _____ it.

3 A _____ me get the door for you.

   B I can _____.

4 A Do you need a hand with that?

   B That's very _____ of you.

5 A I'm getting up. Do you want my seat?

   B Nope, it's all _____.

6 A _____

   B _____

7 A _____

   B _____

2 REAL-WORLD STRATEGY: Imposing on somebody

A **What do the people request? Put the words in the correct order. Write a response either accepting or refusing the request. Then think of two more requests and responses.**

1 I'm / but / sorry / is it / if / OK

   Ana _____ I use your phone for a moment?
Mine is out of battery.

   _____.

2 I / don't / but / mind / rude / would you / to be / mean

   Joe _____ letting me go ahead of you in
line? I only have a few items, and I'm in a rush.

   _____.

3 _____.

   _____.

4 _____.

   _____.

FUNCTIONAL LANGUAGE AND REAL-WORLD STRATEGY

A   **Offer to help the person in the picture. Then write the person's response.**

1

A _____

B _____

2

A _____

B _____

3

A _____

B _____

4

A _____

B _____

B   **Read the situations. Write a request and a response. Use *I'm really sorry to have to ask …* or *I don't mean to be rude …* to make the requests.**

1   Bernardo and Marta are co-workers. Their boss is waiting for their report by 5 p.m. but Bernardo gets a call that his son is sick. Bernardo has to leave. Marta doesn't have to leave.

A _____

B _____

2   Your car has broken down and won't be repaired for a few days. You need a car for a job interview tomorrow. Your neighbor has two cars.

A _____

B _____

6.4 PAINTING SAFER STREETS

1 LISTENING

A 🔊 6.01 **LISTEN FOR GIST** Listen to the conversation about guerilla gardening. Check (✓) the topics that Angela mentions.

What guerilla gardening is	☐
Why she started guerilla gardening	☐
The places she has done guerilla gardening	☐
Other countries where guerilla gardening happens	☐
Some of the problems with guerilla gardening	☐

B 🔊 6.01 **LISTEN FOR DETAIL** Listen again. Write *T* (true) or *F* (false).

1 Greg and Angela both do guerrilla gardening.   F

2 People do guerrilla gardening to improve public spaces.   _____

3 City governments help with guerrilla gardening projects.   _____

4 People can send donations if they want to support guerrilla gardening.   _____

5 Guerrilla gardening groups exist only in North America.   _____

6 Businesses are helping guerilla gardening groups.   _____

2 READING

A **Read about guerrilla gardening in Los Angeles, California. Circle the correct answers.**

Guerrilla gardening started back in the 1970s and has grown into an international movement. In some places, people do it to make public spaces more beautiful; in other places, they do it to grow food. In South Central Los Angeles, it was very difficult in the past to find healthy food. That's why a movement was started to grow vegetable gardens on city property. An organization, L.A. Green Grounds, was formed and started planting fruit trees and vegetables. The gardeners were all volunteers and came from all over the city and many different professions. Green Grounds has helped to change a community. There is plenty more space that could be improved. The city of Los Angeles owns nearly 26 square miles of empty land. That's enough land to plant 725 million tomato plants!

1 Guerrilla gardening started *a few / (many)* years ago

2 In the past, people had to drive far to buy *fast food / healthy food.*

3 L.A. Green Grounds was started in order to *make the community beautiful / grow food.*

4 Volunteers for L.A. Green Grounds *all live / do not all live* in South Central Los Angeles.

5 The city of Los Angeles *owns / does not own* a lot of empty land.

A   Read the report. Find the quotations and circle the phrases that are used to introduce them.
    Then underline the verbs that are used in the phrases.

The city has a lot of empty space that could be used for guerrilla gardening. A recent report by Our Community Together has made a list of the possible places. One of the leaders of the group claimed that "many parts of the city are ugly because nobody takes care of them. Using those spaces to grow plants will make the city more beautiful."

When asked for comment, one resident said, "I think this is an excellent idea. We could start with the Greenwood section of town. Right now it is full of trash. It should be cleaned up."

However, not everybody agrees. One person in city government pointed out that "the city has a lot of needs. The empty space could be used for day-care centers and libraries."

It is true that cities have many needs, but we must accept that having beautiful spaces is one of those needs.

B   Think of an empty space in your town that guerrilla gardening could improve. Write a report about the space. Write about where it is, how big it is, what the space looks like right now, and how it could be changed. Include at least one quotation. You can make up the quotation.

_____

_____

_____

_____

_____

_____

CHECK AND REVIEW

Read the statements. Can you do these things?

UNIT 6	Mark the boxes. ✔ I can do it. ? I am not sure. I can …	If you are not sure, go back to these pages in the Student's Book.
VOCABULARY	☐ use verbs and verb phrases to describe good works.	page 54
	☐ use expressions and different forms of words to talk about good deeds.	page 56
GRAMMAR	☐ use the passive voice in the simple present and simple past.	page 55
	☐ use the passive voice with the modals *can*, *might*, *must*, and *will*.	page 57
FUNCTIONAL LANGUAGE	☐ make, accept, and refuse offers.	page 58
	☐ politely impose on someone.	page 59
SKILLS	☐ write a report about a community project.	page 60
	☐ introduce quotes.	page 60

EXTRA ACTIVITIES

1.5 TIME TO SPEAK Job interviews

A **Which of the following do you think are common interview questions in your country? Write two more interview questions. Why do you think companies ask these questions?**

Where do you see yourself in five years? ☐

Are you married? ☐

What is your greatest weakness? ☐

How much did you make in your last job? ☐

B **How would you answer the questions you checked in exercise A? Write your answers.**

2.5 TIME TO SPEAK Restaurant rescue

A **Think of a restaurant you don't like in your town. Make a list of the things you don't like about it.**

B **Write a letter to the owner offering suggestions on how he/she can improve the restaurant.**

3.5 TIME TO SPEAK A whole new lifestyle

A **Read the beginning of the story below. Complete the story with an expected change in Erika's lifestyle. Go online and find three pictures to help tell the story.**

In college, Erika wanted to travel the world. But a year after Erika just graduated college, she was still living with her parents. She hadn't found a job yet, and she certainly didn't have money to travel. This was _not_ how she had planned her life. So she decided to …

B **Share the photos in the next class. Can anyone guess your story?**

4.5 TIME TO SPEAK Design an ad

A **Look online for an ad written in English. Write a description of the ad.**
- What product is it selling?
- Where does the ad appear? On television? On a website? On a billboard?
- What advertising techniques does it use?
- Do you think the ad is effective? Why or why not?

B **Describe the ad in your next class. Are your classmates familiar with the ad? Do they agree with your opinion of the ad?**

5.5 TIME TO SPEAK A chance meeting

A **Look back at the story on page 52 of the Student's Book. Then answer the questions.**

- What happens in the story?
- What kind of story is it?

B **Choose one of the story types below. Change the details of the story on page 52 of the Student's Book to fit the new story type.**

- coming-of-age story
- mystery
- success story
- tear jerker

C **Present your new story at the next class. Can your classmates guess the new story type?**

6.5 TIME TO SPEAK Your urban art project

A **Go online and find an urban art project somewhere in the world that you think is interesting.**

- What is the project?
- Where is it?
- Who is involved in the project?
- What are the goals of the project?

B **Write a report about the project and bring it to the next class. Explain it and discuss it with the rest of the class.**

The authors and publishers acknowledge the following sources of copyright material and are grateful for the permissions granted. While every effort has been made, it has not always been possible to identify the sources of all the material used, or to trace all copyright holders. If any omissions are brought to our notice, we will be happy to include the appropriate acknowledgments on reprinting and in the next update to the digital edition, as applicable.

Photographs
Key: B = Below, BL = Below Left, BR = Below Right, C = Centre, CL = Centre Left, CR = Centre Right, TC = Top Centre, TL = Top Left, TR = Top Right.

All the photographs are sourced from Getty Images.

p. 2 , p. 53: Hero Images; p. 3: Boris Breuer/The Image Bank; p. 4: maroke/iStock/Getty Images Plus; p. 5: shironosov/iStock/Getty Images Plus; p. 7, p. 55: Jose Luis Pelaez Inc/Blend Images; p. 10: Tony C French/ The Image Bank; p. 11: foxestacado/iStock/Getty Images Plus; p. 12: Eisenhut and Mayer Wien/Photolibrary; p. 13: Alain Schroeder/ONOKY; p. 14: XiXinXing; p. 15: altrendo images/Altrendo; p. 16: petekarici/E+; p. 18: JGI/Blend Images; p. 19: SKA/Cultura Exclusive; p. 20: dardespot/ E+; p. 21: Jon Feingersh/Blend Images; p. 22 (TR): Kwangmoozaa/iStock/ Getty Images Plus; p. 22 (BL): Asia Images Group; p. 23: Yagi-Studio/E+; p. 24: vinhdav/iStock Editorial/Getty Images Plus; p. 26: AfricaImages/ iStock/Getty Images Plus; p. 27: Stewart Bremner/Moment; p. 29: Benjamin Torode/Moment; p. 30: Yellow Dog Productions/The Image Bank; p. 31: SolisImages/iStock/ Getty Images Plus; p. 32 (TR): PhotoAlto/Milena Boniek/Brand X Pictures; p. 32 (CR): Mauro-Matacchione/iStock/Getty Images Plus; p. 34: kzenon/iStock/Getty Images Plus; p. 35: LWA/The Image Bank; p. 37: AntonioGuillem/iStock/Getty Images Plus; p. 38: martin-dm/ E+; p. 39: BakiBG/iStock/Getty Images Plus; p. 40: tommaso79/iStock/ Getty Images Plus; p. 42: Blend Images - KidStock/Brand X Pictures; p. 43, p. 51: Tetra Images; p. 44: fstop123/iStock/Getty Images Plus; p. 45: Mauro-Matacchione/iStock/Getty Images Plus; p. 46: Maskot; p. 47 (TL): ElenaNichizhenova/iStock/Getty Images Plus; p. 47 (CL): Mikael Vaisanen/Corbis; p. 47 (TR): HASLOO/iStock/Getty Images Plus; p. 47 (CR): Jupiterimages/Photolibrary; p. 48: Johner Images.

Front cover photography by Alija/E+.

Audio production by CityVox, New York.

Corpus
Development of this publication has made use of the Cambridge English Corpus (CEC). The CEC is a multi-billion word collection of contemporary spoken and written English. It includes British English, American English, and other varieties. It also includes the Cambridge Learner Corpus, the world's biggest collection of learner writing, developed in collaboration with Cambridge Assessment. Cambridge University Press uses the CEC to provide evidence about language use that helps to produce better language teaching materials. Our Evolve authors study the Corpus to see how English is really used, and to identify typical learner mistakes. This information informs the authors' selection of vocabulary, grammar items and Student's Book Corpus features such as the Accuracy Check, Register Check, and Insider English.